FIFE COUNCIL LIBRARIES

FC540106

KT-578-433

SCHOOLS
LIBRARY
SERVICE

FIFE COUNCIL SCHOOLS	
540106	
PETERS	08-Mar-05
J629.41	£9.99
JEAR	AD

Space Explorer

SPACE TRAVEL

Patricia Whitehouse

www.heinemann.co.uk/library
Visit our website to find out more information about **Heinemann Library** books.

To order:

 Phone 44 (0)1865 888066

 Send a fax to 44 (0)1865 314091

 Visit the Heinemann Bookshop at **www.heinemann.co.uk/library** to browse our catalogue and order online.

First published in Great Britain by Heinemann Library, Halley Court, Jordan Hill, Oxford OX2 8EJ, part of Harcourt Education. Heinemann is a registered trademark of Harcourt Education Ltd.

© Harcourt Education Ltd 2004.
The moral right of the proprietor has been asserted.

All rights reserved. No part of this publication may be reproduced, stored in a retrieval system, or transmitted in any form or by any means, electronic, mechanical, photocopying, recording, or otherwise without either the prior written permission of the Publishers or a licence permitting restricted copying in the United Kingdom issued by the Copyright Licensing Agency Ltd, 90 Tottenham Court Road, London W1T 4LP (www.cla.co.uk).

Editorial: Jilly Attwood and Kate Bellamy
Design: Ron Kamen and Paul Davies
Picture Research: Ruth Blair and Sally Claxton
Illustrator: Jeff Edwards
Production: Séverine Ribierre
Originated by Dot Gradations
Printed and bound in China by South China Printing Company

The paper used to print this book comes from sustainable resources.

ISBN 0 431 11345 9
08 07 06 05 04
10 9 8 7 6 5 4 3 2 1

British Library Cataloguing in Publication Data
Whitehouse, Patricia
Space Travel – (Space Explorer)
629.4'5
A full catalogue record for this book is available from the British Library.

Acknowledgements
The Publishers are grateful to the following for permission to reproduce photographs: Corbis p. **4** (Bettmann); Getty Images pp. **7**, **9**, **10**, **11**; Getty Images/Photodisc pp. **24**, **26**; KPT Power Photos p. **8**; NASA pp. **5**, **6**, **12**, **13**, **16**, **18**, **19**, **20**, **21**, **25**, **27**, **28**, **29**; Science Photo Library pp. **14**, **15**, **17**, **22**, **23** (NASA)

Cover photo reproduced with permission of Science Photo Library.

Our thanks to Stuart Clark for his assistance in the preparation of this book.

Every effort has been made to contact copyright holders of any material reproduced in this book. Any omissions will be rectified in subsequent printings if notice is given to the Publishers.

Disclaimer
All the Internet addresses (URLs) given in this book were valid at the time of going to press. However, due to the dynamic nature of the Internet, some addresses may have changed, or sites may have ceased to exist since publication. While the Author and Publishers regret any inconvenience this may cause readers, no responsibility for any such changes can be excepted by either the Author or the Publishers.

Contents

Words written in bold, **like this,** are explained in the Glossary.

 Find out more about space at www.heinemannexplore.co.uk.

Going to space

On 4 October 1957, Russia launched a rocket into space. The rocket was carrying a **satellite** called Sputnik. This was the first time anything had been sent into space.

Life-size models of the satellite Sputnik were on show around the world.

4

A lot of rocket design and experiments had to be done before people could go into space.

For 21 days, the satellite Sputnik sent its 'beep beep' radio signal to the Earth. It was a success. People started thinking about sending a person to space.

Making rockets

Sending a **satellite** into space was not easy. The Earth's **gravity** pulls everything toward the Earth's centre. Scientists had to make a rocket that could break free from the Earth's gravity.

The scientist Robert Goddard with his rocket in 1926.

Scientists worked on lots of different rocket designs. After many **experiments**, rockets could finally break out from the Earth's gravity.

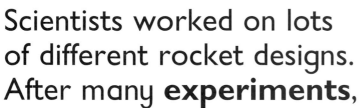

This is a model of the V2 rocket that almost flew into space in 1942.

From 1957 rockets could fly into space. But no one knew if it was safe for a living thing to go into space. Could it survive a rocket launch? Would space make it sick?

Being in space or on the Moon is very different from being on the Earth.

On 3 November 1957, a dog named Laika became the first living thing to go into space. This helped scientists learn about making space travel safe for people.

First person in space

On 12 April 1961, the spacecraft Vostok 1 was launched. A **Russian cosmonaut** called Yuri Gagarin was in it. He became the first person to go into space.

The Vostock 1 flight was controlled by computers on Earth. As Vostock 1 came back to Earth, Yuri jumped out and landed by parachute. His flight had only lasted 108 minutes.

Yuri became a hero when he landed back on Earth.

Early space missions

On 5 May 1961, US **astronaut** Alan Shepard became the second person to go into space. His spacecraft was called Freedom 7. This time, Alan controlled the spacecraft himself.

The **capsules** of the first space missions were tiny. Alan Shepard stayed inside his space capsule when he returned to Earth. It landed in the sea.

capsule

Early space capsules had just enough room for a seat and controls.

Astronauts practised landing vehicles on Earth, ready for going to the Moon.

Once people could get to space, the next challenge was to land on the Moon. **Astronauts** began some difficult training for moon missions.

Engineers worked on designing
safe space shuttles.

Russia and the USA both wanted to
be the first to send a person to the
Moon. Scientists and engineers in both
countries worked on plans and built
equipment. Finally, the first moon
mission was ready.

Moon landing

US **astronauts** Michael Collins, Buzz Aldrin and Neil Armstrong left Earth on 16 July 1969. They travelled for four days and over 350,000 kilometres.

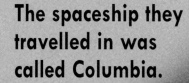

The spaceship they travelled in was called Columbia.

When Armstrong first stepped on to the Moon
he said, 'That's one small step for man, one
giant leap for mankind.'

Neil Armstrong and Buzz Aldrin boarded
a **lunar module**. It left Columbia and
landed on the Moon. Armstrong was the
first man to step on to the Moon.

Travelling on the Moon

On the first three moon landings, **astronauts** explored the Moon on foot. They could not go very far from their **lunar module**.

Astronauts collected rock and dust samples from the Moon.

On the fourth mission to land on the Moon, astronauts took a **Lunar Roving Vehicle**. They could now explore places further away.

A problem in space

Scientists work hard to make sure each space flight is safe. But sometimes things go wrong. On the Apollo 13 mission to the Moon, a tank exploded.

Scientists check all the equipment that will go into space, but something could still go wrong.

Before the Apollo 13 mission, the crew had trained hard to be ready to go into space.

The **astronauts** on the Apollo 13 were running out of air and water. For four days, Mission Control worked hard to help the astronauts get back to Earth safely.

Space shuttle

People wanted to send more **astronauts** and equipment on each mission. Scientists started work on a spacecraft that was big enough for ten astronauts and a **cargo bay**.

The cargo bay of this spacecraft could easily hold a satellite.

A shuttle looks like an aeroplane
and can land on a runway.

On 12 April 1981, the first space
shuttle was launched. Its crew stayed
in space for 2 days.

Space stations

Scientists wanted to know what would happen to people who stayed in space for a long time. They built space stations where **astronauts** could live for months.

The Mir space station was built during the 1970s.

The **Russians** and Americans built their own space stations. Then they worked with fourteen other countries to build an International Space Station. The first part of it was launched in November 1998.

To go to the closest planet, Mars, and back would take more than two years. **Astronauts** need a way to store enough food and water for the long trip.

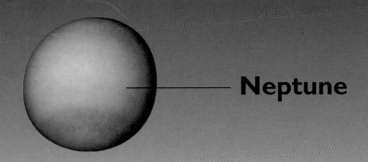

Neptune

Space probes travel across the
solar system, taking pictures and
sending them back to Earth along
the way. In 1997, a robot named
Sojourner landed on Mars. It sent
pictures of Mars to Earth.

Triton

Scientists keep thinking about new ways to travel into space. One idea is a space elevator. This would be like a giant lift that could take people into space.

This is a drawing of what a space elevator might look like.

Spacecraft would ride along the rails of the launch arch before launching into space.

Another idea for a new way to travel into space is a launch arch to help launch spacecraft. Neither the launch arch or the space elevator has been built yet. It may be many years before they are.

Amazing space facts

- It takes about 10.5 minutes to get to space on board a space shuttle.

- The International Space Station can be seen from the Earth. It looks like a tiny point of light moving across the sky.

- Sputnik is **Russian** for '**satellite**'.

- **Astronauts** brought back over 382 kilograms of rock from the Moon.

 Find out more about space at www.heinemannexplore.co.uk.

Glossary

astronaut person who goes to space

capsule part of a rocket that holds astronauts

cargo bay holds satellites and other equipment on a space shuttle

cosmonaut astronaut from Russia

experiment test

gravity a force that pulls objects together

lunar module part of a space shuttle that lands on the Moon

Lunar Roving Vehicle jeep-like car used to travel on the Moon

Russia this country used to be known as the Soviet Union. Its full name is now the Russian Federation.

satellite object that travels around a planet or a moon

space probe spacecraft used to explore space

More books and websites

The Planets (Space Explorer), P. Whitehouse (Heinemann Library, 2004)
The Moon (Space Explorer), P. Whitehouse (Heinemann Library, 2004)
Space Equipment (Space Explorer), P. Whitehouse (Heinemann Library, 2004)

www.esa.int
www.nasa.gov/audience/forkids

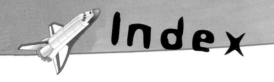

Titles in the *Space Explorer* series include:

Hardback   0 431 11347 5

Hardback   0 431 11348 3

Hardback   0 431 11345 9

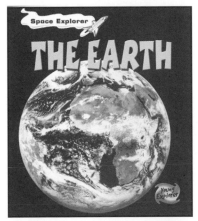

Hardback   0 431 11342 4

Hardback   0 431 11341 6

Hardback   0 431 11344 0

Hardback   0 431 11343 2

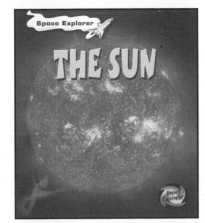

Hardback   0 431 11340 8

Hardback   0 431 11346 7

Find out about the other titles in this series on our website www.heinemann.co.uk/library